Lena

by Heather Clay
illustrated by Mary DePalma

HOUGHTON MIFFLIN HARCOURT
School Publishers

Printed in China

ISBN-13: 978-0-547-02721-0
ISBN-10: 0-547-02721-4

3 4 5 6 7 8 0940 18 17 16 15 14 13 12 11 10

Lena and her family were moving to a new house in a new neighborhood. Lena was sad about moving because she had to leave her pretty garden.

Lena had planted all kinds of flowers and she loved to watch them bloom. She had also planted berry bushes. She gave the plants water and pulled out the weeds. Whenever she saw a sick plant, she tried to make it better.

Lena looked out the window at her garden. She knew that a new family was going to buy the house. She wondered if the new owners would know how to take care of her garden.

She thought hard all night long. Then she had an idea. She wrote some directions and told the new owners just how to care for the garden.

Lena left the directions for the new owners when she moved.

She got right to work planting a garden in her new yard, but she often thought of her old garden.

One night, Lena dreamed about her old garden. In her dream, all the flowers had turned brown.

When Lena woke up, she was worried and upset. "Oh, I hope the new owners are taking good care of my garden!" she cried.

Dear Lena,
I love my new home, and most of all I like the garden.
Thank you for leaving such good directions for taking care of it!
Your friend,
Dolly

A few days later, Lena got a letter and a picture. They made her feel much better.

Dear Dolly,

I am so glad that you like the garden! I have planted a garden in my new yard. The flowers are just starting to bloom.

Your friend,
Lena

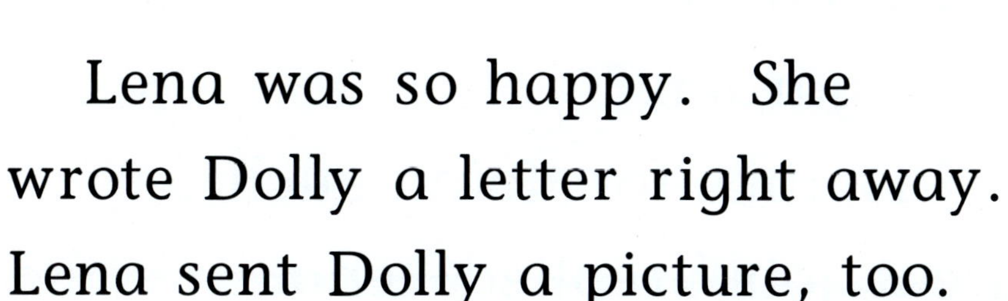

Lena was so happy. She wrote Dolly a letter right away. Lena sent Dolly a picture, too.

The next Saturday, Lena and her family visited the old house. She thought that the garden looked great.

Dolly said, "Thanks for teaching me how to take care of your garden!"

"Thanks for doing such a great job!" replied Lena.

Responding

TARGET SKILL Story Structure

Who is this story about? Where does the story happen? What happens in the story? Make a chart.

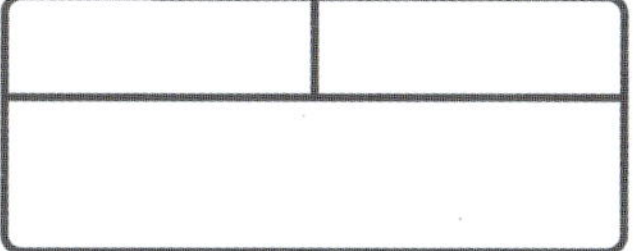

Write About It

Text to World Draw a picture of a garden you would like to visit. Write two sentences about this garden.

better	saw	turned
night	thought	window
pretty	told	

LEARN MORE WORDS

berry	bloom	neighborhood

TARGET SKILL **Story Structure**

Tell the setting, character, and events in a story.

TARGET STRATEGY **Analyze/Evaluate**

Tell how you feel about the text, and why.

GENRE A **fantasy** is a story that could not happen in real life.